Anti-Inflammatory Cookbook

Recipes to Restore Your Health, Heal Your Immune System and Lose Weight Fast

By Jennifer Lawley

ISBN: 1979100810
ISBN-13: 978-1979100816

Table of Contents

The information in the following pages is broadly considered to be a truthful and accurate account of facts and as such any inattention, use or misuse of the information in question by the reader will render any resulting actions solely under their purview. There are no scenarios in which the publisher or the original author of this work can be in any fashion deemed liable for any hardship or damages that may befall them after undertaking information described herein.

Additionally, the information in the following pages is intended only for informational purposes and should thus be thought of as universal. As befitting its nature, it is presented without assurance regarding its prolonged validity or interim quality. Trademarks that are mentioned are done without written consent and can in no way be considered an endorsement from the trademark holder.

Introduction

Inflammation is a great example of the many types of specialized responses the human body has that are, by and large, completely misunderstood. It occurs when the body's internal environment is physically threatened by some form of external factor. This can mean anything from a paper cut, a cold or flu virus, upset stomach after eating spoiled food, to a broken bone due to a fall. If it wasn't for inflammation, such as swelling, for example, all of these things could potentially lead to a deadly infection.

To prevent a small occurrence from turning into something lethal, the body initiates an increase of blood flow to the affected area in order to flood it with white blood cells. Also referred to as leukocytes, these are essentially the body's immunity cells. They are constantly working to destroy harmful invaders, like viruses and bacteria, and keep us disease-free.

Common injuries and infections like these are treated by addressing the symptoms of the affected individual because, under minor circumstances, white blood cells can usually take care of the underlying problem on their own. Maybe you take something for the discomfort, such as ibuprofen or an antacid, or you set the bone so it can heal, but your body does most of the work itself. These ailments are categorized as "acute inflammation", and they are characterized by symptoms which clear up in less than a week.

When undesirable symptoms persist, and continue to affect the sufferer for longer periods (months, even years), it is a result of being continuously exposed to some harmful environmental pathogen which the body's white blood cells cannot eliminate. This occurrence is called "chronic inflammation", which can lead to a vast array of serious and deadly diseases such as ulcerative colitis, diabetes, rheumatoid arthritis, Crohn's disease, asthma, heart disease, Alzheimer's, Parkinson's, and various forms of cancer.

Fortunately, there are natural ways to combat these diseases naturally while simultaneously fighting premature signs of aging, maintaining a healthy body weight, and reducing your level of stress. In this book, we will discuss diet and lifestyle changes that can be made in order to help prevent inflammation in all of its forms as well as how to relieve the symptoms associated with chronic inflammation with delicious recipes and restorative dietary and self-care techniques.

It is important to note that before continuing you take into account that these instructions and suggestions are not meant to replace medical advice provided by your doctor or medical professional in any way. Further, it is not meant to treat or diagnose any disease, illness, malady, or injury. Always consult with your physician before embarking on a new health program, or if you have any questions about a medical condition you may have. That being said, let us begin our journey!

Chapter 1: Effects and Consequences of Chronic Inflammation

Chronic inflammation also called systemic or low-grade inflammation is the underlying cause of most known diseases. In fact, every chronic illness is caused by some type of inflammation. A disease can cause further inflammation and physical problems related to it in turn, but initially, it is also inflammation of some kind that causes the disease. Addressing that initial source of inflammation by targeting its source is the solution to the problem, and preventing systemic inflammation can help us to prevent disease in the first place.

Autoimmune Disease

This type of inflammatory disease can occur when the immune system starts to attack healthy cells which pose no actual threat. This can affect many parts of the body, such as the joints, skin, or internal organs, and is characterized by inflammation of various kinds. There are about 80 different types of autoimmune diseases, and they can be difficult to diagnose because the source of symptoms is often mysterious. It can feel impossible to figure out the cause of the discomfort caused by an autoimmune disease because the pain comes from the immune system performing improperly and not doing what we expect it to. These cases are typically treated with drugs, such as steroids or immunosuppressants, which suppress the immune system and which unfortunately, also have the side effect of making the user more susceptible to infection and illness.

Rheumatoid arthritis is an autoimmune disease which affects the bone joints, such as the fingers, elbows, knees, and even the jaw. The immune system becomes confused and treats healthy joint tissue as a foreign invader to the body. As a result, white blood cells are sent to those joints in order to destroy them. If this internal inflammation goes unchecked, gradual joint deterioration will occur.

Ulcerative colitis and Crohn's disease are both autoimmune diseases affecting the digestive system, but where ulcerative colitis is characterized by inflammation of the inner lining of the colon specifically accompanied by ulcers, those with Crohn's disease can experience inflammation anywhere in the digestive tract. Many symptoms are shared by the two, such as abdominal pain, constipation, diarrhea, fatigue, and weight loss. However, ulcerative colitis, in particular, more commonly causes blood in the stool, while Crohn's disease, which affects a larger portion of the body, can produce symptoms such as sores in the mouth and anal afflictions including ulcers, infections or fissures (tears).

A prime example of autoimmune disease rearing its ugly head in a way that is visible outside the body is psoriasis. Often occurring along with other autoimmune diseases such as the ones previously mentioned, psoriasis is characterized by irritated patches on the skin. An overactive immune system attacks skin cells, causing them to die and requiring the body to replace them. In many cases, new skin cells are being produced faster than the body can get rid of the old ones that are being killed. This causes flaky, thick, red, and often itchy patches on the skin, and the condition is referred to as plaque psoriasis.

Metabolic Syndrome

A precursor to heart disease, stroke, and diabetes, metabolic syndrome refers to a particular set of concurring conditions: high cholesterol, excess fat around the midsection of the body (the waist), high blood sugar, and high blood pressure. These conditions, especially when any number of them occur together, can drastically increase the likelihood of these deadly diseases. Metabolic syndrome is also linked to obesity, although it is not clear which causes which, as cases differ widely. Either way, systemic inflammation is always linked with these occurrences.

Diabetes is a disease related to the insulin hormone, which turns the sugar from carbohydrates into energy to be used by the body. The body becomes less able, or unable, to produce insulin or respond to it, depending on the type of diabetes a person has. Type 1 diabetes, on the other hand, is an autoimmune condition, and it occurs when the immune system attacks cells in the pancreas, resulting in the body's decreased or diminished ability to make insulin. Type 2 diabetes is characterized by the inability of the body to use glucose and insulin normally. As a result, excess glucose ends up in the blood, causing high blood sugar levels.

Heart disease comes in many forms and affects sufferers in a number of different ways. Heart attacks occur when blood flow is restricted and cannot reach part of the heart, resulting in the death of some number of cells that make up the heart muscle. Heart failure, or the heart's lack of ability to send enough blood through the body, happens gradually as a result of high blood pressure, problems with the valves of the heart, diabetes, coronary artery disease (a hardening and narrowing of the arteries due to high cholesterol and plaque build-up therein), or a predisposition due to a birth defect affecting the heart. High cholesterol in the blood is a major contributor to all of these conditions.

Strokes occur as a result of inflammation of the brain and can cause permanent disability and in many cases, death. It is typically caused by systemic inflammation of the arteries related to heart disease, but specifically, a stroke happens when part of the brain does not receive adequate blood flow. Without enough oxygen, the brain cells in this area are killed. As a result, a stroke can render a person unable to use that area of the brain, losing control over whatever activities are governed by it, such as speech or muscle movement. Once a stroke happens, the immune system kicks into high gear and sends white blood cells to repair the damage. The inflammation that results, although its initial purpose is to heal the brain, causes further harm to the brain and can lead to additional strokes.

Age-related Disease

The aging process may also be contributed to by low-grade inflammation. Although it is not known for sure if inflammation causes aging, if aging causes inflammation, or if both are true, aging and inflammation are closely related. To understand how, we need to look at physical aging as characterized by a decline in the function of the body's systems, and how the function of those systems is affected by systemic stress. Inflammation is a form of stress, and when the body encounters stress, it taxes the ability of the body and mind to perform in general. This includes repairing and generating tissue, which is integral to maintaining supple skin and organ function (including the brain), among many other aspects of aging.

Alzheimer's disease, also known as dementia, involves the loss of memory and other cognitive functions. Age is the most prominent risk factor, but many people suffer from it who are not elderly. This type of occurrence is referred to as early-onset Alzheimer's. Both are degenerative, meaning that the conditions worsen over time. Damaged nerve cells inside the brain are the cause of Alzheimer's, blocking the pathway of communication between nerve cells which is needed for them to survive. When these cells die and this communication is cut off, the information those cells are trying to deliver throughout the brain is stopped short, leading to memory loss. This cell death is caused by inflammation in the brain.

Parkinson's disease, another degenerative disease often associated with age, is marked by a loss of the brain's ability to control the movement of the muscles. This can affect writing, speaking, and potentially a person's ability to walk without assistance. Linked to a low level of dopamine in the brain (which is a type of neurotransmitter), Parkinson's results from a diminishing of the brain's ability to transmit signals in areas of the brain, which are in charge of muscle movement. This disease, like Alzheimer's, is linked to inflammation because inflammation causes damage to brain cells in these areas.

Cancer

Inflammation has a well-studied link to cancer. In fact, tumors have been found to contain immune cells. A tumor attracts immune cells in order to bring in blood and oxygen to keep it alive, and these immune cells also release chemicals that promote growth in the tumor and assist it in damaging and consuming healthy cells that surround it. Since immune cells are the major player in systemic inflammation, which involves an increase in immune cells and their activity, systemic inflammation creates an opportune environment for abnormal cells to create tumors, which can ultimately become lethal.

These are just a handful of the dangerous consequences of uncontrolled inflammation inside the body. However, there are ways to fight these diseases and keep your cells healthy and growing. The foods you choose to eat and the activities you engage in can directly enhance your body's ability to maintain a healthy inflammatory response. Taking an honest approach to your diet and lifestyle and making a shift toward positive change could save your life!

Chapter 2: The Anti-Inflammatory Diet

The foods we choose to eat are intrinsic to the health of our body's systems. You truly are what you eat, and making better food choices is the first step to gaining control of systemic inflammation. Making the switch to heart-healthy fats, absorbable, high-quality proteins, and minimally-processed and gut-friendly carbohydrates while including plenty of fresh fruits and vegetables and dietary fiber will keep you on the right track on the road to lifelong health.

Fat Sources

In the past, we have been led to believe that fats are the enemy of a healthy diet. Illnesses such as high cholesterol, heart disease, and obesity were all supposed to be a result of a high-fat diet, and the solution was thought to be a reduction of dietary fat. Now we know that fat in the diet does not necessarily lead to fat on your waistline or excess cholesterol in your arteries. Responsible for maintaining healthy skin, absorbing vitamins and minerals from the diet, and providing energy, fats are a necessary part of a healthy diet. In moderation, fat can be an anti-inflammatory powerhouse when we choose the right sources.

Trans fat, found in hydrogenated or partially-hydrogenated oil, is produced by heating a fat or oil in the presence of hydrogen. It is highly processed and therefore difficult for the body to recognize and break down properly. As a result, consuming trans fats can lead to building up of a form of cholesterol called LDL (low-density lipoprotein). LDL cholesterol creates plaque inside the arteries, which leads to heart disease. Foods containing trans fats should be avoided altogether.

In general, deep-fried foods should be avoided in order to reduce inflammation. This is because of a process called oxidation, which occurs when oil either goes rancid due to age, light exposure, and/or oxygen exposure or is burned or heated for a prolonged period or repeatedly, like in a fryer used at a restaurant. When a fat is oxidized, it not only loses its health benefits, but it also promotes inflammation in the body. Some experience high blood pressure or hypertension to some degree even directly after consuming oxidized fat.

Certain oils, in particular, should be avoided due to their higher risk of oxidation. Examples of oils to look out for and avoid are canola, cottonseed, soybean, vegetable oil (which is often mostly soybean oil), sunflower, and corn. These oils, also known as industrial seed oils, are unstable, meaning that the temperature required to oxidize the fatty acids within is very low. This means that whether your potato or corn chips are baked or fried if one of these oils is listed in the ingredients, they contain oxidized fat.

Make the switch from these hazardous types of fat to healthy, inflammation-fighting fats such as those found in coconut oil, olive oil, wild-caught fish, nuts, seeds, and avocado. Animal fat sources, such as red meat, eggs, and dairy (butter, milk, and cheese), should be used sparingly, and only high-quality sources should be sought out. Seek out products made from grass-fed or free-range animals to get the right quantity of omega 3 and 6 fats. When these are present in the wrong ratio, as is the case with factory-farmed livestock and products made from animals that are not fed their natural diet and not allowed to live in their natural surroundings, it can contribute to inflammation when consumed by humans.

Finding the right balance of omega fatty acids are integral to maintaining a healthy inflammatory response. There are three different types of omega fats: omega-6, omega-3, and omega-9. Both omegas 6 and 3 are both essential fatty acids, which means that we as humans cannot produce them on our own, and we need to find them via our diet. These two fatty acids need to be consumed in balance with one another. That is not to say that if you eat a cookie made with soybean oil (which contains a large amount of omega-6), you can balance it out by eating some salmon or walnuts (which both contain omega-3). You need to choose foods that contain the proper ratio of omega-6 and omega-3 fatty acids within them for your body to process and absorb these fats properly.

Omega-9 fatty acids, on the other hand, are non-essential, meaning that the human body naturally produces it. However, it is found in a number of healthy fat sources such as walnuts, cashews, almonds, peanuts, avocado, and olive oil. Generally, omega-3 fats are found in fish sources which are oily such as anchovies, sardines, salmon and mackerel, as well as flaxseed, walnuts, and chia seeds, whereas omega-9 and omega-6 fats are found mainly in plant sources like nuts and seeds. This is why it is important to include a balance of wild-caught fish and nuts and seeds in your diet to maintain a healthy balance of all three omega fatty acids in the body.

Protein

Getting an adequate amount of protein in your diet is critically important for keeping inflammation to a minimum. Protein supports the growth of muscles and joints and contributes to the healing and repair of damaged tissue, which is a common occurrence among people with overactive immune systems or increased levels of systemic inflammation. However, not all proteins are used by the body in the same way, and it's important to make sure you are getting the kind of protein your body needs.

If you choose to abstain from animal products, make sure you are consuming the best possible plant-based protein sources. Beans and legumes can be an adequate source of protein for those on a vegetarian or vegan diet, but only when they are prepared from a dried state by first soaking and then either cooking or sprouting. Preparing beans with this method unlocks the maximum amount of absorbable nutrients, particularly when they are sprouted. There are defense mechanisms within these foods that prevent the human body from absorbing nutrients such as vitamins, minerals, and protein, leaving us with mostly carbohydrates and fiber. These defenses are known as phytic acid, phytates or "anti-nutrients", and they can be removed partially by soaking before cooking and almost entirely removed by sprouting.

Although there are ways of preparing plant-based protein sources to make their protein more available to us, animal products are the easiest way to get adequate protein in the diet. If you prefer a meat-free way to get more protein into your diet, consider supplementing your diet with eggs from pasture-raised, free-range chickens. Try finding a local farm that you know produces quality eggs and treats their livestock humanely, and source from there. Locally-sourced foods, in general, are not only better for your body because they are fresher and contain more nutrients than those found on the grocery store shelf that have traveled hundreds of miles, they also help your local economy and allow you to feel more connected to the food on your plate.

High-quality meat, seafood, eggs, and dairy products can also be a healthy part of an anti-inflammatory diet. These foods are the best possible sources of protein for the human body. Again, always choose products made from naturally and humanely raised animal sources, and avoid any type of factory-farmed animal products and farm-raised seafood. These animals are raised in conditions so different from their natural environment that the ratio of nutrients we absorb from them is out of balance, and can contribute to inflammation. Quality animal-based protein sources may have a higher price tag than conventional sources, but you will be following a mostly plant-based diet from here on out, and these foods are meant to supplement this diet rather than form the basis of it. This is an investment in your health, so think of the money you will be saving on medical bills later on.

As for meat consumption, opt for fish and lean cuts of chicken without the skin. Red meat and pork can cause inflammation due to high levels of omega-6 fats. Remember that must be in balance with omega-3 fatty acids, and when red meat and pork is consumed in too large a quantity or too regularly, it can throw the ratio of these fats out of balance and contribute to inflammation. Eliminate all forms of processed meat altogether, like bacon, ground meat and hamburger, sausage, deli meat, and jerky for the same reason, and also because they typically contain preservatives which inhibit digestion and cause oxidative cell damage and aging.

You may also want to try reducing your dairy intake to control inflammation. Lactose and dairy intolerance is highly prevalent among human populations from various regions, and if you are one of the people who suffer from such an intolerance without knowing it, you may be consuming a food you are in fact allergic to. Food allergies are a major contributing factor to systemic inflammation, and the only way to know for sure if the inflammation you are experiencing is due to a food intolerance is to eliminate it. Try abstaining from dairy products such as milk, cheese, butter, and yogurt for a couple of weeks to one month to see if any of your undesirable symptoms subside, then try reintroducing it. If you have a negative reaction, you most likely have a dairy sensitivity and should avoid it entirely.

Fiber

Fiber is integral for the optimal gut and digestive health, which forms the basis of a healthy, functioning body and mind. It moves food and nutrients through the digestive tract to be absorbed and eliminated properly, and is also beneficial for the health of your gut and feeding the beneficial bacteria that live there. Fiber content is something to seek out in the foods you choose not only to maintain your overall health, but also to help keep inflammation at bay.

A correlation has been found between people who have adequate amounts of fiber in their diets and lower levels of types of systemic inflammation which leads to diabetes, heart disease, and autoimmune disease. One reason for this could be that a fiber-rich diet can assist in maintaining a healthy weight, which acts as a key player reducing the risk of inflammatory disease. Also, the fact that fiber supports a healthy culture of bacteria inside the gut means that it helps support a healthy immune system, and thus a healthy immune response, which can lead to lowered levels of inflammation. Because it is unclear if fiber specifically is what provides this benefit, or if it's the nutrients found in the foods that contain it, it's best to obtain fiber from food sources rather than fiber supplements.

Carbohydrates

When it comes to carbohydrates or carbs, focus on those which are complex, meaning that they do not break down quickly into sugar. Simple carbs, on the other hand, which turn into sugar much more rapidly, will spike your blood sugar and can contribute to inflammation. Examples of complex carbs include whole grains, beans, legumes, and vegetables, whereas simple carbs like refined flours, sugar, and baked goods should be avoided.

Carbohydrates play a significant role in blood sugar regulation and heart health. Scientists used to believe that it was fat that contributed to heart disease more than any other food, but now we know that certain types of carbs are the culprit. Refined, or simple carbs found in processed foods such as bread, cakes, and pasta, are processed very quickly by the body and turned into sugar. This spikes your blood sugar, giving you a burst of energy, only to make you crash and feel tired soon thereafter. This is an eating pattern that has been linked to diabetes and heart disease.

Complex carbs, on the other hand, are minimally processed and are digested more gradually. This type of carb also turns into sugar, but much more slowly. The sugar is released gradually into the bloodstream, giving you a milder form of sustained energy that is more tolerable to your digestive system and metabolism as well as being more nourishing the systems of the body that regulate stress and mood. A diet focused on complex carbs also helps you to manage your weight because they help you to feel fuller and more nourished throughout the day.

Fresh Fruits and Vegetables

Your best sources of dietary fiber combined with vitamins and minerals are vegetables and fruit. Freshness and seasonality are important aspects to look for in order to find the best quality and nutritional value. When choosing fruits, look for options that are lower in sugar while being higher in fiber in order to reap the most benefits. High-sugar fruits have their own benefits, but they should be eaten sparingly so as not to spike your blood sugar. These types of fruits are known as "low-glycemic", and some examples are pears, apples, blueberries, raspberries, and blackberries. High-fiber vegetables include beans, lentils, spinach, avocado, broccoli, peas, artichokes and brussels sprouts.

Fruits and vegetables also contain phytonutrients (literally meaning "plant nutrients") which help to fight inflammation. These nutrients support the body's systems by nourishing them with vitamins and minerals while also helping to detoxify them. Dark, leafy greens and bitter-tasting vegetables, in particular, have a detoxifying effect on different organ systems. Heavily pigmented fruits and vegetables contain antioxidants, which scavenge the free radicals inside the body that contribute to aging and death of cells, effectively keeping our cells alive.

It is always best to choose locally grown fruits and vegetables. Freshness is key; the fresher the food is, the more nutrients it contains. After a plant is cut from its life source (the ground, or the tree, for example), its nutritional content begins to gradually diminish. For this reason, it is always best to choose foods from local sources, which have not traveled a great distance to reach your plate. When you purchase locally produced foods, you are not only doing your body a favor but you are also supporting your local farmers and economy.

Chapter 3: Creating Healthy Habits

Hydrate

Getting in the habit of drinking plenty of water and fluids is one of the most important changes you can make when trying to reduce inflammation. By moving toxins through your system to be eliminated, adequate hydration helps to detoxify your body. Fluid intake can also reduce untimely food cravings, or feel the need to snack when your body does not require calorie intake. Hydration is also key to nourishing joint and muscle tissue, which is made up 50 to 60 percent water. Always choose pure, filtered water, as tap water often contains heavy metals and chemicals that can be harmful to your body and contribute to inflammation.

From day to day, our bodies accumulate toxins from our environment. The air we breathe, our food, and even sometimes the clothes we wear often contain some level of toxins. Although harmless in small quantities, these toxins can build up in your system and your body's cells can become congested, which can lead to a decrease in their function. When our cells are not functioning optimally, they can age more rapidly and also lead to systemic inflammation as a result.

Water intake can also help to remove excess weight from the body by reducing the occurrence of food cravings when you are not actually hungry, while also addressing digestive problems and preventing constipation. When you feel hungry even though it is not the time to eat a meal, try drinking some water before you decide to have a snack. Your body may just need some hydration and is telling you to consume in order to fill that void. Drinking water will also keep your digestive tract lubricated, and thus more able to move food through and process nutrients efficiently. This also contributes to healthy elimination by preventing constipation and ensuring that waste is properly removed from the body.

Detoxify

Keeping toxins in the body to a minimum will help you to maintain healthy inflammation levels and allow your body to function at its best. Stick to organic foods without any added chemicals, preservatives, pesticides or antibiotics to avoid build-up of these dangerous toxins in your system in the first place. Exercise is another important way to remove excess waste from the body, especially when you work up a sweat and then rehydrate afterward by drinking plenty of water. Regular exercise trains your body to remove waste more efficiently, even when you are sitting still.

A three-day detox is a great way to kick-start your anti-inflammatory diet. Try a juice cleanse, which may get your inflammation down to a baseline by giving your digestive system a break while loading you up with plenty of nutrients to revitalize you. You will need to invest in a juicer to get the freshest possible juice, which will give you the most available nutrients, and also be able to customize your recipes to your needs. Burdock root and dandelion greens are both cleansing tonics that have a powerful detoxifying action on the liver and kidneys and are a great addition to supercharge a juice recipe. Use low-sugar fruit as your bases, such as green apple and berries, to keep your blood sugar at a healthy level. Drink four to six small glasses of juice per day, spread out over a few hours in between to keep cravings to a minimum. Adding water so you can enjoy a larger glass to sip on for a longer period could also help prevent food cravings.

Alkalize

Having too much acid-forming food in your diet can promote inflammation, so make sure to balance your diet with plenty of alkalizing foods. Your body functions best when it maintains a healthy pH value, and this value can be thrown off by consuming too many foods that are either acid-forming or alkalizing. Acid-forming foods can be particularly problematic for those with inflammatory conditions, so it is important to make sure you are not consuming too much of them while at the same time consuming a roughly equal amount of alkalizing foods to balance them out and maintain a healthy pH level inside the body.

Examples of alkalizing foods include vegetables (especially potatoes, carrots, celery, and spinach), fruits (especially cherries, bananas, and apricots), nuts, and seeds. Consuming adequate amounts of these foods will help to boost your immune system and regulate a healthy immune response while protecting your cells from oxidation. Although counter-intuitive, vinegar, lemon, and lime juice have an alkalizing effect on the body even though they themselves are highly acidic. This is because the byproduct that is created after we metabolize these foods is made up of different properties than the foods themselves.

A few examples of acid-forming foods are beans and legumes, peas, alcohol, grains, and animal products such as eggs, dairy (with the exception of cultured yogurt), fish, meat, and poultry. When these foods are digested and metabolized, they leave behind an acidic residue. When accumulated to a large amount, this acidity in the body can lead to high susceptibility to illness and disease. Keep in mind, however, that these foods can be healthy for you in moderation. Your goal should be to balance them with roughly twice the amount of alkalizing foods. For example, for each acid-forming food you eat every day, try to incorporate two alkalizing foods.

Sleep

Among the most important factors when trying to reduce inflammation is adequate rest. When you sleep, your body recovers from the previous day and repairs damaged tissues. If you don't allow your body to fully recharge before getting up and putting it back to work, you are burning the candle at both ends. It is only a matter of time before your body decides it's time to make you stop when you might not be ready to. This can happen in the form of an illness such as inflammatory disease.

Sleep may be one of the most difficult aspects of a healthy lifestyle for many people to consistently maintain. We expect a lot of work from our bodies each day, and it can be easy to neglect the body's needs when the needs outside of ourselves are constantly demanding us to keep going. You must bear in mind that when it comes to our physical selves, we will only reap what we sow. You will only get from your body what you give to it, so no matter what, make time to get at least 8 hours of sleep each night. If you are sick, you may require more than that or even a short nap during the day in addition. Listen to your body; if you feel tired, take a moment to rest, even if only to close your eyes for a few minutes. If you don't feel better, get to a quiet place as soon as you are able and catch some Zzzz's.

Manage Stress

Stress appears in many forms. It can motivate us to make a positive change like you have done by choosing this book. It can also mean feeling overwhelmed, overworked, anxious or exhausted. Sometimes stress can creep up on us, and we don't realize we are experiencing it until it has already begun to take a physical toll. Because it is an unavoidable part of everyday life, the key to preventing stress from becoming harmful is to find a way to manage it and adapt to it. Making time for self-care is immensely important, and it will help you manage stress and keep it from causing you harm.

Chronic stress can be extremely detrimental to your overall health. Unlike typical everyday stress, chronic stress persists over a long period of time and can cause anxiety, muscle discomfort, difficulty sleeping, decreased immune function and high blood pressure. All of these symptoms lead to some form of systemic inflammation over time and can contribute to inflammatory conditions. Unhealthy ways of dealing with stress, such as overeating or over-exercising, make things even worse.

There are different approaches you can take to manage stress. First, make sure you get plenty of sleep and go to sleep at the same time each night. A regular sleeping and waking schedule alone can relieve a significant amount of stress. Also, eliminate the use of electronic screens and lights before bedtime. If you keep a television in the bedroom, consider removing it and instead go to bed a little bit early and read for a while to calm the brain and prepare it for sleep. This will lessen the possibility of disruption in your sleep cycle during the night and ensure a restful sleep.

Getting regular restorative exercise will also help to reduce stress. Exercise increases the production of endorphins in the brain, which relieves anxiety and depression. It also strengthens the body's systems so that they can more easily adapt to the physical effects of stress. A healthy body contributes to a healthy mind, and mindful exercise is an integral part of keeping both body and mind healthy and functioning at their best. Exercising mindfully means maintaining body awareness during exercise, rather than mindlessly muscling through a workout. Yoga is a great way to practice mindful exercise, and doing yoga may inform your own exercise routine and make it work more for your benefit.

A wide range of health benefits can be gained from meditation, one of which is a reduction in stress levels. Meditation focuses your attention on the present moment, which is especially helpful during times of stress when your mind darts around and circles around worrisome thoughts. One way to meditate is to simply focus on your breathing and allow your thoughts to pass through you, without holding onto any of them. If you make time every day to meditate, even just fifteen minutes, you will notice a positive change in your overall mood and energy level.

Chapter 4: Kitchen equipment

High-Speed Blender

Unlike a standard blender, a high-speed blender has the ability to pulverize food items that are difficult to break down such as raw beets and whole nuts. This type of blender costs a bit more than a standard blender, but it will be able to tackle just about any recipe and a high-quality model will last a very long time if cared for properly.

Juicer

Juicing is a great way to maximize your nutrient intake while giving your digestion a break. When you use a centrifugal juicer, the juice from fresh vegetables and fruits is extracted by grinding up the foods and forcing them through a sieve, leaving the pulp behind. Alternatively, you can use a masticating juicer, which requires that the food be cut up into small pieces first, and the result is a juice with a bit more pulp. Which juicer you choose is a matter of personal preference.

Food processor

Investing in a food processor will save you loads of food preparation time. No more mincing garlic and chopping vegetables by hand; just remove the parts you don't want to consume, place what you want to chop inside the work bowl and pulse the blade until your desired consistency is reached. You can let the machine do most of the work for you and save your joints the unnecessary stress.

Spiralizer

Spiral-cut vegetables such as carrots, beets, sweet potatoes and zucchini squash make excellent substitutes for pasta and noodles made from processed grains and starches. Using a spiralizer is also a great way to supercharge your diet with nutrients you might not normally be getting otherwise. It will also save you money in the long run because you can make almost any starchy vegetable into noodles of various shapes and sizes.

Chapter 5: Recipes

Now that you have resolved to make a positive change for your health, here are some delicious recipes to keep you on the right track. These recipes have been chosen for their versatility; they can all be modified to include your favorite ingredients, and you can feel free to swap them for any listed ingredients you choose.

Breakfasts, Juices, and Smoothies

Gluten-free crepes

You will need:

3 tablespoons of coconut oil, melted and divided (1 for the pan, 2 for the batter)
1 cup of gluten-free flour, all-purpose
1 tablespoon of maple syrup
1/4 teaspoon of sea salt
1/2 cup of water
1/2 cup of non-dairy milk (almond, rice, coconut, etc.)
1 teaspoon of vanilla extract
2 eggs

Method:

1. Combine the maple syrup, water, milk, vanilla, and eggs in a medium-sized bowl. Using a whisk, combine thoroughly.

2. Gradually add the flour and whisk together.

3. While whisking, slowly pour 2 tablespoons of coconut oil. Whisk thoroughly until it's completely smooth. If

the oil starts to solidify, microwave the mixture in ten second intervals, whisking in between, until uniform consistency is achieved.

4. Over your medium heat setting, add the remaining coconut oil to a medium-sized pan.

5. One-third of a cup at a time, pour the batter into the pan. For each crepe, as soon as you put the batter into the hot pan, tilt and swirl the batter around to create an even, thin layer.

6. Cook each crepe for about two minutes. When the bottom of the crepe turns golden, flip the crepe and do the same for the other side.

7. Repeat steps 5 and 6 for each crepe until all the batter has been used.

8. Fill each crepe with your choice of fresh fruit and Coconut Whipped Cream (see recipe in Desserts).

Asparagus and Mushroom Frittata

You will need:

3 tablespoons of basil, chopped
1/2 a cup of cheese, shredded (mozzarella, cheddar, or Monterey jack)
1/4 cup of water
7 eggs
1/2 cup of tomatoes, chopped
1 cup of asparagus, sliced into 1 inch sections
1 cup of mushrooms, thickly sliced
2 teaspoons of olive oil
Black pepper and sea salt to taste
Red pepper flakes to taste

Method:

1. Heat your oven to 350° F.
2. Using a medium heat setting, heat a medium-sized oven-safe pan. Add enough oil to coat the pan.
3. Sauté the mushrooms and asparagus until mushrooms release moisture and the asparagus is somewhat soft.
4. Add the tomatoes and cook for one minute, then remove the pan from the heat.

5. In a different bowl, whisk together the eggs, water, pepper, and salt. Then mix in the cheese and basil.
6. Pour the egg mixture over the vegetables in the pan. Make sure the vegetables are evenly distributed in the egg mixture.
7. Place the pan in the center of the oven and bake the frittata for about 15-20 minutes, until slightly set.
8. Slice and serve.
9. To store, remove from the pan, wrap in aluminum foil, and refrigerate.

Apple Spice Muffins

Yield: About 8 muffins

You will need:

Half a cup of almond meal
Half a cup of buckwheat flour
1/4 cup of brown rice flour, superfine grind
1/4 cup of raw cane sugar
2 tablespoons of arrowroot starch
2 teaspoons of baking powder
1 tablespoon of ground flaxseed
1/2 teaspoon of cinnamon
3/4 teaspoon of ground ginger root
1/4 teaspoon of nutmeg
One pinch of clove
1/4 teaspoon sea salt
1 apple, cored and finely chopped
1 large egg, room temperature
6 tablespoons + 2 teaspoons of non-dairy milk, room temperature (almond or rice)
1/4 cup of coconut oil, melted
1 teaspoon of vanilla extract

Method:

1. Preheat your oven to 350° F.
2. Line a muffin tin with paper liners.
3. In a medium-sized bowl, whisk the dry ingredients. Add to this mixture the apple and mix to coat each piece.
4. In a separate similarly sized bowl, combine the second set of ingredients (wet) and whisk thoroughly to combine. **Note:** None of these ingredients can be cold, or the coconut oil will solidify and you will have trouble mixing it all together.
5. Add the wet ingredients to the dry and stir until thoroughly mixed and no dry pockets remain.
6. Scoop the batter into the muffin liners, filling them each almost all the way to the top.
7. Sprinkle with a little bit of raw cane sugar and bake for 20-25 minutes, or until an inserted toothpick can be removed cleanly.
8. Set the muffin tin on a rack to cool.
9. Store in a tightly closed container or wrap individually and freeze when they are completely cool.

Gingerbread Oatmeal

Yield: 2 servings

You will need:

1 cup of rolled oats, gluten-free and organic
2 cups of water
1 teaspoon of ground ginger root
2 teaspoons of cinnamon
1/4 teaspoon of nutmeg
1/4 teaspoon of allspice
1/4 teaspoon of clove
Two pinches of sea salt
1 - 2 tablespoons of maple syrup, to taste
Non-dairy milk (almond or coconut) for drizzling
Optional: sliced fresh bananas, berries, or apples

Method:

1. Boil the water.
2. Add oats, spices, and salt, then lower heat to a low simmer.
3. Cover and simmer for about ten minutes.

4. When the oats has absorbed all the liquid, stir in maple syrup and top with milk and fruit if desired. Serve immediately.

Green smoothie

Yield: 2 servings

You will need:

2 ripe bananas
1 cup of non-dairy milk (almond, rice, or coconut)
½ cup of raw almonds
4 cups of fresh baby spinach
1 teaspoon of ground cinnamon
One large pinch of ground nutmeg
2 tablespoons of ground flaxseed OR whole chia seed

Method:

1. Blend everything in your high-speed blender until completely smooth.
2. Serve immediately.

Pink Smoothie

Yield: 2 servings

You will need:

1 cup of tart cherry juice

1 cup of strawberries, sliced

1/2 cup of red beets, chopped

About a half-inch piece of fresh ginger, grated

2 tablespoons of raw honey

1/2 teaspoon of ground cinnamon

4-5 ice cubes

Method:

1. Blend everything in your high-speed blender until completely smooth.
2. Serve immediately.

Golden Smoothie

Yield: 2 servings

You will need:

2 cups of water
2 cups of frozen pineapple
2 cups of frozen mango
1 cup of coconut milk, canned
2 teaspoons of ground turmeric
2 teaspoons of freshly grated ginger

Method:

1. Blend everything in your high-speed blender until completely smooth.
2. Serve immediately.

Chocolate Peanut Butter Banana Smoothie

Yield: 2 servings

You will need:

1 cup of water

2 ripe bananas

1/4 cup of cocoa powder

2 tablespoons of raw honey

2 tablespoons of peanut butter

4-5 ice cubes

Method:

1. Blend everything in your high-speed blender until completely smooth.
2. Serve immediately.

Green Juice

Yield: 2 servings

You will need:

About a two-inch piece of fresh ginger
1 lemon, peeled
1 cup of fresh spinach
Half of a green apple
1 cup of pineapple
Half a cucumber
4 stalks of celery

Method:

1. Process all the ingredients together through a juicer.
2. Serve immediately.

Carrot Ginger Juice

Yield: 2 servings

You will need:

1 medium zucchini squash

2 pears, cores removed

1 lemon, peeled

About a two-inch piece of ginger

4 carrots

2 medium green apples

Method:

1. Process all the ingredients together through a juicer.
2. Serve immediately.

Cooling Fennel Juice

Yield: 2 servings

You will need:

3 sprigs of spearmint

2 pears

2 medium oranges, peeled

1 lemon, peeled

1 medium bulb of fennel

1/2 cup of coconut water, no sugar added

Method:

1. Process all the ingredients together through a juicer.
2. Serve immediately.

Golden Turmeric Juice

Yield: 2 servings

You will need:

6 one-inch pieces of fresh turmeric root

2 pears

2 lemons, peeled

About a one-inch piece of fresh ginger root

3 stalks of celery

3 carrots

2 medium green apples

Method:

1. Process all the ingredients together through a juicer.
2. Serve immediately.

Purple Juice

Yield: 2 servings

You will need:

About a one-inch piece of fresh ginger root

6 carrots

6 stalks of celery

1 medium green apple

1 red beet, 3inch diameter

1 lime, peeled

1 large wedge of purple cabbage

Method:

1. Process all the ingredients together through a juicer.
2. Serve immediately.

Warming Spiced Apple and Carrot Juice

Yield: 2 servings

You will need:

Two one-inch pieces of fresh turmeric root
2 pears
2 lemons, peeled
About a one-inch piece of fresh ginger
3 stalks of celery
2 medium green apples

Method:

1. Process all the ingredients together through a juicer.
2. Serve immediately.

Snacks

Guacamole

Yield: 1-½ cups

You will need:

2 medium ripe avocados, pitted and diced (keep one of the pits)
1 large clove of Garlic
¼ cup of diced red onion
3 tablespoons fresh lime juice
½ cup of fresh cilantro, chopped
Sea salt and black pepper, to taste
Optional: 2 tablespoons of diced fresh jalapeño

Method:

1. Combine everything in a medium-sized bowl.
2. Using a fork, roughly mash everything together and stir thoroughly to combine.
3. Serve immediately with plantain chips or fresh vegetables such as carrot sticks or bell pepper slices. Store leftovers in a tightly sealed container in the

refrigerator. Putting the avocado pit in the container as well, will help to prevent browning.

Indian-Spiced Hummus

Yield: About 1 ½ cups

You will need:

1 ½ cups (or 15 oz. can) cooked chickpeas, cooking liquid (or can liquid) reserved
¼ cup of tahini, almond, or cashew butter
1 lime
2 large cloves of garlic, crushed and peeled
1 tablespoon of Indian curry seasoning (or a blend of ground turmeric, ginger, mustard, cumin, cardamom, fenugreek and coriander)
Sea salt, black pepper and cayenne, to taste
2 tablespoons of olive oil

Method:

1. Put the chickpeas and garlic cloves in a food processor and pulse to form a crumbly consistency.
2. Add the juice from the lime, tahini, or nut butter, and seasonings and process. Gradually add the cooking liquid or can liquid until the mixture starts to become smooth.

3. Add the olive oil and process until completely smooth.
4. Serve with fresh sliced vegetables such as carrots, cucumbers, bell peppers, and gluten-free crackers, and store in a tightly sealed container in the refrigerator.

Jalapeño Poppers

Yield: 3 servings

You will need:

1/3 cup of prepared salsa
1 tablespoon of grated parmesan
9 large jalapeño peppers, halved lengthwise and de-seeded
2 tablespoons of fresh basil, chopped
¼ cup of roasted red bell peppers, chopped
2 green onions, green parts sliced
1/3 cup of shredded cheddar cheese
¾ cup ricotta cheese
¼ cup of cooked quinoa or rice

Method:

1. Preheat your oven to 375° F.
2. In a medium-sized bowl, place cheddar, ricotta, onion, red pepper, basil, and quinoa or rice and mix.
3. Stuff each Jalapeño half with the above mixture and top with parmesan.
4. Bake on the center oven rack for 18-22 minutes, until the jalapeños are soft.

5. Serve topped with salsa, or use it for dipping. Refrigerate the leftovers.

Thai Shrimp Lettuce Wraps

Yield: 3 servings (6 rolls)

You will need:

1 tablespoon of fresh basil

½ cup of scallions, green parts chopped

¾ cup of shredded carrots

¾ cup of cucumbers, sliced into matchsticks

7 oz. wild-caught shrimp, cooked and chopped

12 firm lettuce leaves

1 tablespoon of lime juice, fresh

2 tablespoon of gluten-free hoisin sauce or 1 tablespoon of soy sauce (gluten-free) or tamari

1 teaspoon of sesame oil

Method:

1. Combine everything except the lettuce in a large mixing bowl.
2. Double up the lettuce leaves. Using two leaves per roll, fill each lettuce cup with filling, dividing evenly, and roll up to seal.

3. Serve, and store leftovers in the refrigerator, individually wrapped.

Zucchini Fries

Yield: 2 servings

You will need:

1/3 cup of tomato sauce
Coconut or olive oil, to coat (spray is best)
1 tablespoon of non-dairy milk (rice, almond, etc.)
1 egg
Black pepper and sea salt, to taste
1 tablespoon of parmesan, grated
2 tablespoons of almond meal
1 tablespoon of gluten-free all-purpose flour
1/2 lb of zucchini, sliced into 3inch sticks

Method:

1. Heat the oven to 425° F and line a sheet pan with a baking parchment.
2. Fill a large zip-top freezer bag with half of the almond meal and half of the flour.
3. Fill another bag with the remaining almond meal and flour, parmesan, pepper, and salt.

4. In a medium-sized bowl, place the egg and non-dairy milk and mix thoroughly using a whisk.
5. Working in batches, toss zucchini sticks in the flour mixture in the first bag.
6. Add the leftover flour mixture from the first bag to the second bag.
7. Dip coat zucchini sticks in the egg mixture and transfer to the second bag with flour and seasonings.
8. Spread the zucchini sticks on the baking sheet and spray with oil (or drizzle).
9. Bake for about 25 minutes, until zucchini is soft and outside is crispy.
10. Serve immediately with warmed tomato sauce for dipping.

Trail mix

Yield: 4 cups

You will need:

1/2 cup of dark chocolate chips (sugar-free or low-sugar)
½ cup of raisins
½ cup of dried pineapple, mango or papaya chunks
½ cup of sunflower seeds
½ cup of pumpkin seeds
¾ cup of walnuts, chopped
¾ cup of peanuts or cashews
¼ teaspoon of sea salt
½ teaspoon of ground cinnamon
One pinch of ground nutmeg

Method:

1. If any of your nuts are raw, toast them in a pan using the medium heat setting, stirring frequently until they become fragrant. Remove from the pan and let them cool.
2. Put everything together in a mixing bowl and mix.

3. Serve, and store leftovers in a tightly sealed container away from heat or direct light.

Pickled Eggs and Beets

Yield: 5 servings

You will need:

5 beets, peeled
5 eggs, hard-boiled and peeled
Half of a small red onion, sliced thinly
1 cup of apple cider vinegar, raw and unfiltered
3 cups of water
2 tablespoons of raw honey
½ teaspoon of sea salt
¼ teaspoon of black pepper
Optional: pinch of ground cinnamon and ground or whole clove

Method:

1. Using a medium-sized saucepan, boil beets and water using a medium-high heat setting. Reduce to a simmer and cook for about 25 minutes, until beets have become soft.

2. Remove beets from the water and set aside until completely cool. Reserve the cooking water and let cool.
3. When the beets have cooled and can be handled, slice into discs or wedges and set aside.
4. When the water has cooled to room temperature, add honey, vinegar, salt, pepper, and spices and stir to dissolve.
5. In a large glass container or in separate glass jars, divide the eggs and beets evenly and cover with liquid.
6. Seal tightly and refrigerate for at least 2 days to marinate.
7. Serve, and keep leftovers in the refrigerator for up to a month. The liquid can be reused to pickle a second batch of eggs.

Lunch

Fennel, Celery, and Apple Salad

Yield: 3 servings

You will need:

2 stalks of celery, sliced thinly
1 apple, sliced thinly
1 half-pound bulb of fennel, bulb sliced thinly and leaves included
2 tablespoon of fresh lemon juice
2 tablespoons of feta cheese
1 tablespoon of extra virgin olive oil
Black pepper and sea salt, to taste

Method:

1. Put everything in a large mixing bowl and combine.
2. Serve immediately or refrigerate to store.

Jicama, Avocado and Orange Salad

Yield: 4 servings

You will need:

4 cups of jicama, cubed
¼ teaspoon of sea salt
¼ cup of fresh orange juice
2 tablespoons of fresh lime juice
2 oranges, peeled and sectioned
1 ripe avocado, sliced
3 tablespoons of fresh cilantro, chopped
Optional: .5 lb. of chicken breast, cooked

Method:

1. Combine jicama, salt, lime orange juices in a medium bowl. Stir and marinate 2-4 hours.
2. Add the remaining ingredients and top with the chicken.
3. Serve immediately and store leftovers in the refrigerator.

Italian White Bean Stew

Yield: 6 servings

You will need:

½ cup of quinoa
¼ cup of fresh basil, chopped
1 carrot, chopped
4 cloves of garlic, minced
2 celery stalks, diced
3 cups of fresh tomato, chopped
1 medium yellow onion, diced
2 tablespoons of olive oil
6 cups of cannellini beans, canned or cooked
5 cups of water or free-range chicken broth
½ teaspoon of sea salt, to taste
½ teaspoon of black pepper

Method:

1. Using a large-sized soup pot, heat the oil over the medium setting. Add garlic, onion, carrot, and celery and sauté until slightly softened. Add the tomato, then

cook for 15 minutes, or until the liquid is released and everything is saucy.

2. Add the beans, water or broth, pepper, and salt, and boil. Bring the heat down to medium-low and cook for 20 minutes, or until the beans are soft.
3. Add the quinoa and continue to simmer over medium-low for 15 minutes, or until the quinoa grains pop open and their tails come out.
4. Take off the heat and stir in the basil. Mix to combine and allow to cool for about 15-20 minutes.
5. Serve, and store cooled leftovers in the refrigerator.

Sweet Potato soup

Yield: 4 servings

You will need:

1 tablespoon of coconut oil
1 cup of broth (free-range chicken or vegetable)
1 medium yellow onion
4 cloves of garlic, chopped
2 tablespoons of fresh dill, chopped (extra for garnish)
1 red bell pepper, chopped
2 carrots, chopped
2 cups of fresh baby spinach
1 large sweet potato
1 medium avocado
1 ½ cups of lentils, canned or cooked
Black pepper and sea salt, to taste
Raw cashews, chopped, for garnish

Method:

1. In a large-sized soup pot over a medium heat, add the oil. When the oil starts to become hot, add the garlic

and onion and cook for 30 seconds, or until they start to brown.

2. Add the sweet potato, bell pepper, and carrots and mix to coat.
3. Add the spinach and cook for about a minute, stirring constantly until wilted.
4. Add the lentils and broth or stock and boil.
5. Bring the heat down to a simmer and cook for about 15 minutes until everything is heated through.
6. Allow to cool slightly, then working in partial amounts at a time if necessary, process in a high-speed blender. Add the avocado and dill and blend until creamy and no chunks remain.
7. Serve topped with cashews and dill, and store leftovers in the refrigerator once completely cool.

Beet Salad Sandwiches or Lettuce Wraps

Yield: 4 servings

You will need:

2 tablespoons of ground flaxseed
2 tablespoons of fresh lemon juice
2 tablespoons of almonds or cashews, chopped
1 large carrot, grated
1 large apple, chopped
2 cloves garlic, minced
1 large raw beet, grated
Black pepper and sea salt, to taste
2 tablespoons of fresh dill, chopped
Lettuce leaves or salad greens
Optional: 4 whole-grain or gluten-free bread slices

Method:

1. Put everything except for the lettuce and bread in a large bowl and mix.
2. Chill, tightly sealed, for a few hours before serving to marinate.

3. Serve as wraps using lettuce, on a bed of greens as a salad, or on bread with lettuce or greens as a sandwich. Store separately in the refrigerator.

Raw Pad Thai

Yield: 4 servings

You will need:

¼ cup of almond or peanut butter
1 tablespoon of fresh lime juice
2 tablespoons of tamari
1 tablespoon of raw honey or maple syrup
1 clove of garlic, minced
½ teaspoon of ginger root, freshly grated
Optional: Hot sauce or crushed/ground cayenne pepper

½ cup of cauliflower, chopped
½ cup of purple cabbage, shredded
1 scallion, green parts chopped
1 large carrot, cut into spirals
1 medium zucchini, cut into spirals
½ cup mung bean sprouts

Method:

1. Combine the ingredients from the first group in a medium bowl and whisk to combine. This will be used for the sauce.
2. Use a vegetable spiralizer to cut the carrots and zucchini into spirals. Combine these and everything else except for the mung bean sprouts in a large bowl.
3. Mix thoroughly and top with mung bean sprouts to serve. Store leftovers tightly sealed in the refrigerator.

Dinner

Puttanesca with Zucchini Noodles

Yield: 2 servings

You will need:

14 oz. whole, peeled tomatoes, canned
¼ cup Kalamata or black olives, sliced
2 anchovy fillets, oil reserved
2 tablespoons of parsley, chopped (fresh)
½ teaspoon of crushed red pepper
¼ teaspoon black pepper
¼ teaspoon of sea salt
1 tablespoon of capers
1 tablespoon of olive oil
1 clove of garlic, minced
1 large zucchini squash, cut into spirals

Method:

1. Put the oil into a large-sized pan over your medium heat setting on the stove. Add the anchovies and garlic

and continue cooking until anchovies soften and blend with the oil.

2. Add the tomatoes to the pan one at a time, crushing them with your hands. Add enough sauce from the can to create a sauce that is not too liquid.
3. Add a small amount of anchovy oil to taste.
4. Add olives, capers, parsley, salt, and pepper and continue cooking for about 10-15 minutes, until the sauce becomes thick.
5. Add the zucchini noodles and toss to combine. Remove from the heat.
6. Serve, and store leftovers tightly sealed in the refrigerator once completely cool.

Wild Rice Burrito Bowl

Yield: 2 servings

You will need:

(For the sauce)

2 medium ripe avocados, pitted

¼ cup of olive oil

1½ cup of non-dairy milk (almond, rice or coconut)

¼ cup of fresh cilantro leaves

1 scallion, green parts chopped

2 cloves garlic, crushed and peeled

2 tablespoons of fresh lime juice

½ teaspoon of lime zest

¼ teaspoon of sea salt

¼ teaspoon of black pepper

¼ teaspoon of ground cumin

Red pepper flakes, to taste

(For the base)

1 cup of cooked wild rice

3 cups of salad greens or romaine lettuce, chopped

(Toppings)

Chickpeas or black beans, tossed in taco seasoning and oven-roasted at 375° F until soft

Roasted corn kernels, fresh or frozen

Prepared salsa, Pico de Gallo, or fresh tomatoes

Red onion, chopped

Method:

1. Place everything listed for the sauce into your high-speed blender and process until no chunks remain.
2. Store in a small sealed container in the refrigerator until ready to use.
3. Place ½ cup of wild rice into each of two bowls and top with salad greens or lettuce.
4. Arrange the remaining ingredients around the edge of the bowl and drizzle with the sauce.
5. Serve immediately. Store all leftovers in separate containers in the refrigerator.

Root Vegetable and Kale Stew

Yield: 6 servings

You will need:

Pumpkin seeds, for garnish

¼ cup of fresh cilantro leaves, chopped

2 tablespoons of lemon juice

2 cups of kale leaves, chopped

2 medium carrots, chopped

2 medium peeled Yukon gold potatoes, cubed

2 medium peeled sweet potatoes, cubed

3 tablespoons of tomato paste

4 cups of vegetable broth

1 large yellow onion, chopped

2 cloves garlic, chopped

2 tablespoons of coconut oil

1 medium parsnip, chopped

1 teaspoon of ground cumin seed

½ teaspoon of ground ginger root

½ teaspoon of ground cinnamon

1 teaspoon of sea salt

¼ teaspoon of ground cayenne pepper

Black pepper

Method:

1. Over your medium heat setting on the stovetop, place an oil soup pot (large). Cook onion until slightly soft.
2. Add the parsnips and toss to coat. Cook until they start to brown, about 5 minutes.
3. Add both potatoes and carrots, garlic, spices, and tomato paste.
4. Add broth and boil, then simmer using a medium-low heat setting and cook for about 20 minutes, until vegetables are soft.
5. Add lemon juice and kale and cook until kale is slightly softened, less than 5 minutes.
6. Remove from the heat and serve garnished with pumpkin seeds. Once completely cool, store in the refrigerator.

Oven Roasted Salmon and Brussels Sprouts

Yield: 3 servings

You will need:

1 lb of wild-caught salmon fillets
¼ cup of white wine
3 cups of brussels sprouts, sliced in half lengthwise
½ teaspoon of black pepper
2 tablespoons of extra virgin olive oil
½ teaspoon of sea salt
1 tablespoon of fresh rosemary, chopped
7 cloves garlic, roughly chopped
Lemon wedges for garnish

Method:

1. Heat oven to 450° F.
2. Using a small bowl, mix olive oil, rosemary, garlic, pepper, and sea salt.
3. In a large roasting pan, toss the brussels sprouts and 3 tablespoons of the oil mixture. Cook on the center rack for 7 minutes, then stir and cook for another 7 minutes, or until the brussels sprouts are slightly soft.

4. To the remaining oil and herb mixture, add the white wine.
5. Remove the pan from the oven and place salmon on top of the brussels sprouts. Pour the wine mixture over the salmon.
6. Bake for another 10 minutes, or until salmon is cooked through.
7. Garnish with lemon wedges and serve. Store leftovers in the refrigerator.

Arroz con Pollo (Spanish Chicken with Rice)

Yield: 2 servings

You will need:

1 cup of chicken breast, cooked and sliced
1 ½ cup of fresh green beans, chopped
1 tablespoon of fresh oregano, chopped
Half of a bay leaf
½ cup of vegetable broth
1/3 cup water
¼ cup tomato sauce, canned
Half of a medium yellow onion, diced
1 teaspoon of olive oil
1 clove garlic, minced
½ cup of cooked brown rice

Method:

1. Place the oil in a large pan over your medium heat setting.
2. Add the garlic and onion and cook until the onion starts to soften.

3. Add the water, tomato sauce, bay leaf, broth, salt, pepper, and oregano. Stir and bring to the boil.
4. Add the green beans and cook on a low heat setting for about 8 minutes, or until green beans are tender.
5. Add the chicken and rice. Stir to coat and cook for another minute or two until everything is heated through and no liquid remains.
6. Remove from the heat and serve drizzled with olive oil. Store leftovers in the refrigerator.

Dessert

Coconut Whipped Cream

Yield: 8 servings

You will need:

1 teaspoon of vanilla extract
Liquid Stevia, to taste
2 cans of coconut milk, full-fat
1 tablespoon of tapioca starch

Method:

1. Chill both coconut milk cans overnight in the back of your refrigerator on the bottom shelf (the coldest spot).
2. Open the cans and pour off the liquid. You can reserve this for use in a smoothie.
3. Scrape solidified coconut cream into a food processor. Pulse to break up large chunks.
4. Add the vanilla and Stevia to taste and pulse to combine.

5. Add the tapioca and process as briefly as you can until everything becomes fluffy and light. Over-processing can lead to a grainy texture. If this happens, melt it in the microwave and chill again until solid.
6. If your coconut cream remains too liquid to whip, chill it again overnight and process again when it has become solid.
7. Serve on top of a smoothie, as a crepe filling, or on top of any dessert.

Pumpkin Pie Smoothie

Yield: 2 servings

You will need:

About half of a 15 oz. can of pumpkin
About half of a can of full-fat coconut milk (13.5 oz)
1 tablespoon of ground flaxseed or whole chia seed
4-5 ice cubes
1 teaspoon of ground cinnamon
About a half-inch piece of fresh ginger root, grated
¼ teaspoon of nutmeg
¼ teaspoon of allspice
One pinch of clove
2 teaspoons of vanilla extract
3 tablespoons of raw honey or maple syrup
Optional: Two scoops of whey protein

Method:

1. Put everything into your high-speed blender and run until completely smooth.
2. Serve immediately.

Creamy Blueberry Freezer Pops

Yield: 6 freezer pops

You will need:

6 small paper cups
6 Popsicle sticks
3 cups of plain yogurt (dairy or non-dairy)
2 tablespoons of raw almonds
1 cup of blueberries, fresh or frozen

Method:

1. Place the berries and almonds into the work bowl of a food processor.
2. Pulse to form small pieces.
3. Add the yogurt and process until smooth.
4. Divide the mixture equally into each of the 6 cups and place a Popsicle stick into each center.
5. Place the cups into freezer and allow to freeze completely overnight.
6. Peel off the paper cups and serve.

Apples with Cinnamon Tahini Sauce

Yield: 1 serving

You will need:

1 medium Apple
2 tablespoons of tahini
About 2 tablespoons of water
¼ teaspoon of ground cinnamon
¼ teaspoon of vanilla extract

Method:

1. Core the apple and slice into bite-sized wedges.
2. To a small bowl, add tahini then add the water a small amount at a time, stirring vigorously between additions with a spoon, until a light, fluffy consistency is achieved.
3. Add the vanilla, cinnamon, and salt and stir to combine.
4. Serve the apples immediately with tahini sauce on the side for dipping.

Conclusion

Although dealing with the inflammatory disease can be harrowing, the lifestyle and dietary changes you make to combat it will change your whole life for the better. Your body will learn to dislike the foods and habits that are harmful, and instead, you will, naturally crave what your body needs. This is because your body intrinsically knows what it needs, and the key to getting back your health lies in tuning in and listening to what your body is trying to tell you. If you wait too long to make these changes, your body may need to shout in order to get your attention, and this often happens in the form of disease which is difficult to reverse.

When it comes to disease prevention, the key lies within your body. Starting from the inside, even when dealing with a seemingly external problem, will not only ensure that you get to the root of the ailment but also help to keep your other body systems in check at the same time. It all starts in the gut. From there, a chain reaction results, and even small changes inside the body can have far-reaching consequences, visibly and invisibly, down the road. Maintaining gut health is integral to ensuring that your body can deal with whatever the future may throw your way. A healthy diet, along with adequate hydration, proper sleep habits, healthy stress-management and regular, mindful exercise, will keep you on the right path and empower you to be your very best self in mind, body, and spirit.

Printed in Great Britain
by Amazon

36161148R00057